Maya Angelou

Maya Angelou has been waitress, singer, actress, dancer, activist, editor, filmmaker, writer, mother, and now inaugural poet. She first thrilled the world with her autobiography *I Know Why the Caged Bird Sings*. This was followed by *Gather Together in My Name*, *Singin' and Swingin' and Gettin' Merry Like Christmas*, *The Heart of a Woman* and *All God's Children Need Travelling Shoes*. Virago also publish two works of prose, *Wouldn't Take Nothing for my Journey Now* and her most recent book, *Even the Stars Look Lonesome* (1998). She has also written several collections of poetry: *And Still I Rise*, *Just Give Me a Cool Drink of Water 'Fore I Diiie* and *I Shall Not Be Moved*. In 1993, Maya Angelou wrote her historic poem *On the Pulse of Morning*, for the Inauguration of President Clinton. All are included in *The Complete Collected Poems* (1995).

Maya Angelou now has a life-time appointment as Reynolds Professor of American Studies at Wake Forest University in North Carolina.

KT-572-859

ALSO BY MAYA ANGELOU

I Know Why the Caged Bird Sings
Gather Together in My Name
Singin' and Swingin' and Gettin' Merry Like Christmas
The Heart of a Woman
All God's Children Need Travelling Shoes
And Still I Rise
Just Give Me a Cool Drink of Water 'Fore I Diiie
I Shall Not Be Moved
On the Pulse of Morning
The Complete Collected Poems
Oh Pray My Wings Are Gonna Fit Me Well
Shaker, Why Don't You Sing?
Phenomenal Woman
A Brave and Startling Truth
Even the Stars Look Lonesome

WOULDN'T TAKE NOTHING FOR MY JOURNEY NOW

MAYA ANGELOU

A *Virago* Book

Published by Virago Press 1995
Reprinted 2000
First published by Virago Press in 1994

First published in the USA by Random House Inc. 1993

Copyright © Maya Angelou 1993

A portion of this work was originally published in the December 1992
issue of *Essence* Magazine

The moral right of the author has been asserted.

All rights reserved.
No part of this publication may be reproduced,
stored in a retrieval system, or transmitted, in any form
or by any means, without the prior permission in writing
of the publisher, nor be otherwise circulated in any form of binding
or cover other than that in which it is published and
without a similar condition including this condition
being imposed on the subsequent purchaser.

A CIP catalogue record for this book
is available from the British Library

ISBN 1 86049 140 5

Printed and bound in Great Britain
by Clays Ltd, St Ives plc

Virago Press
A Division of
Little, Brown and Company (UK)
Brettenham House
Lancaster Place
London WC2E 7EN

This book
is dedicated to
Oprah Winfrey
with immeasurable love.

ACKNOWLEDGMENTS

My thanks to Susan Taylor, editor in chief of *Essence* magazine, and Marcia Gillespie, editor in chief of *Ms.* magazine, who persuaded me that some lessons in living, which I had learned over many years, would be of use if featured in a magazine article.

My tender love to Rosa Johnson, "The Black Rose." My tender love to Araba Budu-Arthur Bernasco.

Wisdom was created before all things,
and prudent understanding from Eternity.

—Book of Acts of the Apostles

CONTENTS

WOULDN'T
TAKE
NOTHING
FOR MY
JOURNEY NOW

IN
ALL
WAYS
A WOMAN

In my young years I took pride in the fact that luck was called a lady. In fact, there were so few public acknowledgments of the female presence that I felt personally honored whenever nature and large ships were referred to as feminine. But as I matured, I began to resent being considered a sister to a changeling as fickle as luck, as aloof as an ocean, and as frivolous as nature.

The phrase "A woman always has the right to change her mind" played so aptly into the negative image of the female that I made myself a victim to an unwavering decision. Even if I made an inane and stupid choice, I stuck by it rather than "be like a woman and change my mind."

Being a woman is hard work. Not without joy and even ecstasy, but still relentless, unending work. Becoming an old female may require only being born with certain genitalia, inheriting long-living genes and the fortune not to be run over by an out-of-control truck, but to become and remain a woman command the existence and employment of genius.

The woman who survives intact and happy must be at once tender and tough. She must have convinced herself, or be in the unending process of convincing herself, that she, her values, and her choices are important. In a time and world where males hold sway and control, the pressure upon women to yield their rights-of-way is tremendous. And it is under those very circumstances that the woman's toughness must be in evidence.

She must resist considering herself a lesser version of her male counterpart. She is not a sculptress, poetess, authoress, Jewess, Negress, or even (now rare) in university parlance a rectoress. If she is the thing, then for her own sense of self and for the education of the ill-informed she must insist with rectitude in being the thing and in being called the thing.

A rose by any other name may smell as sweet, but a woman called by a devaluing name will only be weakened by the misnomer.

She will need to prize her tenderness and be able to display it at appropriate times in order to prevent toughness from gaining total authority and to avoid becoming a mirror image of those men who value power above life, and control over love.

It is imperative that a woman keep her sense of humor intact and at the ready. She must see, even if only in secret, that she is the funniest, looniest woman in her world, which she should also see as being the most absurd world of all times.

It has been said that laughter is therapeutic and amiability lengthens the life span.

Women should be tough, tender, laugh as much as possible, and live long lives. The struggle for equality continues unabated, and the woman warrior who is armed with wit and courage will be among the first to celebrate victory.

PASSPORTS
TO
UNDERSTANDING

Human beings are more alike than unalike, and what is true anywhere is true everywhere, yet I encourage travel to as many destinations as possible for the sake of education as well as pleasure.

It is necessary, especially for Americans, to see other lands and experience other cultures. The American, living in this vast country and able to traverse three thousand miles east to west using the same language, needs to hear languages as they collide in Europe, Africa, and Asia.

A tourist, browsing in a Paris shop, eating in an Italian *ristorante*, or idling along a Hong Kong street, will encounter three or four languages as she negotiates the buying of a blouse, the paying of a check, or the choosing of a trinket. I do not mean to suggest that simply overhearing a foreign tongue adds to one's understanding of that language. I do know, however, that being exposed to the existence of other languages increases the perception that the world is populated by people who not only speak differently from oneself but whose cultures and philosophies are other than one's own.

Perhaps travel cannot prevent bigotry, but by demonstrating that all peoples cry, laugh, eat, worry, and die, it can introduce the idea that if we try to understand each other, we may even become friends.

THE
SWEETNESS
OF CHARITY

The New Testament informs the reader that it is more blessed to give than to receive. I have found that among its other benefits, giving liberates the soul of the giver. The size and substance of the gift should be important to the recipient, but not to the donor save that the best thing one can give is that which is appreciated. The giver is as enriched as is the recipient, and more important, that intangible but very real psychic force of good in the world is increased.

When we cast our bread upon the waters, we can presume that someone downstream whose face we will never know will benefit from our action, as we who are downstream from another will profit from that grantor's gift.

Since time is the one immaterial object which we cannot influence—neither speed up nor slow down, add to nor diminish—it is an imponderably valuable gift. Each of us has a few minutes a day or a few hours a week which we could donate to an old folks' home or a children's hospital ward. The elderly whose pillows we plump or whose water pitchers we refill may or may not thank us for our gift, but the gift is upholding the foundation of the universe. The children to whom we read simple stories may or may not show gratitude, but each boon we give strengthens the pillars of the world.

While our gifts and the recipients should be considered, our bounty, once decided upon, should be without concern, overflowing one minute and forgotten the next.

Recently I was asked to speak before a group of philanthropists and was astonished at their self-consciousness. The gathered donors give tens of millions of dollars annually to medical research, educational development, art support, and social reform. Yet to a person they seemed a little, just a

little, ashamed of themselves. I pondered their be-
havior and realized that someone had told someone
that not only was it degrading to accept charity but
it was equally debasing to give it. And sad to say,
someone had believed that statement. Hence,
many preferred to have it known that they dispense
philanthropy rather than charity.

I like charitable people and like to think of
myself as charitable, as being of a generous heart
and a giving nature—of being a friend indeed to
anyone in need. Why, I pondered, did the benefactors not feel as I?

Some benefactors may desire distance from
the recipients of their largess because there is a
separation between themselves and the resources
they distribute. As inheritors or managers of fortune rather than direct earners, perhaps they feel
exiled from the gifts; then it follows that they feel
exiled from the recipient.

It is sad when people who give to the needy
feel estranged from the objects of their generosity.
They can take little, if any, relish from their acts of
charity; therefore, are generous out of duty rather
than delight.

If we change the way we think of charity, our

personal lives will be richer and the larger world will be improved. When we give cheerfully and accept gratefully, everyone is blessed. "Charity . . . is kind; . . . envieth not; . . . vaunteth not itself, is not puffed up."

NEW
DIRECTIONS

In 1903 the late Mrs. Annie Johnson of Arkansas found herself with two toddling sons, very little money, a slight ability to read and add simple numbers. To this picture add a disastrous marriage and the burdensome fact that Mrs. Johnson was a Negro.

When she told her husband, Mr. William Johnson, of her dissatisfaction with their marriage, he conceded that he too found it to be less than he expected, and had been secretly hoping to leave and study religion. He added that he thought God was calling him not only to preach but to do so in Enid, Oklahoma. He did not tell her that he knew a minister in Enid with whom he could study and who had a friendly, unmarried daughter. They parted amicably, Annie keeping the one-room house and William taking most of the cash to carry himself to Oklahoma.

Annie, over six feet tall, big-boned, decided that she would not go to work as a domestic and leave her "precious babes" to anyone else's care. There was no possibility of being hired at the town's cotton gin or lumber mill, but maybe there was a way to make the two factories work for her. In her words, "I looked up the road I was going and back the way I come, and since I wasn't satisfied, I decided to step off the road and cut me a new path." She told herself that she wasn't a fancy cook but that she could "mix groceries well enough to scare hungry away and from starving a man."

She made her plans meticulously and in secret. One early evening to see if she was ready, she placed stones in two five-gallon pails and carried them three miles to the cotton gin. She rested a little, and then, discarding some rocks, she walked in the darkness to the saw mill five miles farther along the dirt road. On her way back to her little house and her babies, she dumped the remaining rocks along the path.

That same night she worked into the early

hours boiling chicken and frying ham. She made dough and filled the rolled-out pastry with meat. At last she went to sleep.

The next morning she left her house carrying the meat pies, lard, an iron brazier, and coals for a fire. Just before lunch she appeared in an empty lot behind the cotton gin. As the dinner noon bell rang, she dropped the savors into boiling fat and the aroma rose and floated over to the workers who spilled out of the gin, covered with white lint, looking like specters.

Most workers had brought their lunches of pinto beans and biscuits or crackers, onions and cans of sardines, but they were tempted by the hot meat pies which Annie ladled out of the fat. She wrapped them in newspapers, which soaked up the grease, and offered them for sale at a nickel each. Although business was slow, those first days Annie was determined. She balanced her appearances between the two hours of activity.

So, on Monday if she offered hot fresh pies at the cotton gin and sold the remaining cooled-down pies at the lumber mill for three cents, then on Tuesday she went first to the lumber mill presenting fresh, just-cooked pies as the lumbermen covered in sawdust emerged from the mill.

For the next few years, on balmy spring days, blistering summer noons, and cold, wet, and wintry middays, Annie never disappointed her customers, who could count on seeing the tall, brown-skin woman bent over her brazier, carefully turning the meat pies. When she felt certain that the workers had become dependent on her, she built a stall between the two hives of industry and let the men run to her for their lunchtime provisions.

She had indeed stepped from the road which seemed to have been chosen for her and cut herself a brand-new path. In years that stall became a store where customers could buy cheese, meal, syrup, cookies, candy, writing tablets, pickles, canned goods, fresh fruit, soft drinks, coal, oil, and leather soles for worn-out shoes.

Each of us has the right and the responsibility to assess the roads which lie ahead, and those over which we have traveled, and if the future road looms ominous or unpromising, and the roads back uninviting, then we need to gather our resolve and, carrying only the necessary baggage, step off that road into another direction. If the new choice is also unpalatable, without embarrassment, we must be ready to change that as well.

STYLE

Content is of great importance, but we must not underrate the value of style. That is, attention must be paid to not only what is said but how it is said; to what we wear, as well as how we wear it. In fact, we should be aware of all we do and of how we do all that we do.

Manners and a respect for style can be developed if one is eager and has an accomplished teacher. On the other hand, any observant person can acquire the same results without a teacher simply by carefully watching the steady march of the human parade.

Never try to take the manners of another as

your own, for the theft will be immediately evident and the thief will appear as ridiculous as a robin with peacock feathers hastily stuck on. Style is as unique and nontransferable and perfectly personal as a fingerprint. It is wise to take the time to develop one's own way of being, increasing those things one does well and eliminating the elements in one's character which can hinder and diminish the good personality.

Any person who has charm and some confidence can move in and through societies ranging from the most privileged to the most needy. Style allows the person to appear neither inferior in one location nor superior in the other. Good manners and tolerance, which are the highest manifestation of style, can often transform disaster into good fortune. Many people utter insults or disparaging remarks without thinking, but a wise or stylish person takes the time to consider the positive as well as negative possibilities in each situation. The judicious response to a gibe can disarm the rude person, removing the power to injure.

This is not another admonition to turn the other cheek, although I do think that that can be an effective ploy on certain occasions. Rather, this is an encouragement to meet adverse situations with the intent and style to control them. Falling into an entanglement with brutes will usually result in nothing more conclusive than a stimulated nervous system and an upset digestive tract.

IN
THE SPIRIT

Spirit is an invisible force made visible in all life. In many African religions there is the belief that all things are inhabited by spirits which must be appeased and to which one can appeal. So, for example, when a master drummer prepares to carve a new drum, he approaches the selected tree and speaks to the spirit residing there. In his prayer he describes himself, his experience, and his expertise; then he explains his intent. He assures the spirit that he will remain grateful for the gift of the tree and that he will use the drum only for honorable purposes.

I believe that Spirit is one and is everywhere

present. That it never leaves me. That in my igno-
rance I may withdraw from it, but I can realize its
presence the instant I return to my senses.

It is this belief in a power larger than myself
and other than myself which allows me to venture
into the unknown and even the unknowable. I
cannot separate what I conceive as Spirit from my
concept of God. Thus, I believe that God is Spirit.

While I know myself as a creation of God, I
am also obligated to realize and remember that
everyone else and everything else are also God's
creation. This is particularly difficult for me when
my mind falls upon the cruel person, the batterer,
and the bigot. I would like to think that the mean-
spirited were created by another force and under
the aegis and direction of something other than my
God. But since I believe that God created all things,
I am not only constrained to know that the oppres-
sor is a child of God, but also obliged to try to treat
him or her as a child of God.

My faith is tested many times every day, and
more times than I'd like to confess, I'm unable to
keep the banner of faith aloft. If a promise is not
kept, or if a secret is betrayed, or if I experience
long-lasting pain, I begin to doubt God and God's
love. I fall so miserably into the chasm of disbelief

that I cry out in despair. Then the Spirit lifts me up again, and once more I am secured in faith. I don't know how that happens, save when I cry out earnestly I am answered immediately and am returned to faithfulness. I am once again filled with Spirit and firmly planted on solid ground.

IS ANYONE
EVER
TOO MUCH?

There are a few misguided wits who think they are being complimentary when they declare a woman is "too much." While it is admirable and desirable to be enough, only masochists want to be "too much." Being, claiming, or accepting the status allows others to heap responsibilities upon the back of the "too much" woman, who naturally is also referred to as "super." "Super Woman" and "Earth Mother."

The flatterer, for that is what the speaker means to be, exposes himself as a manipulator who expects to ingratiate himself into "Earth Mother's" good graces, so that she will then take his burdens upon her and make his crooked ways straight.

When the complimenter is confronted, he will quickly disavow any scurrilous intent and with hurt feelings will declare, "I meant 'too much' to be a sign of my appreciation. I don't see how you could misread my meaning. You must be paranoid."

Well, yes. A certain amount of paranoia is essential in the oppressed or in any likely targets of oppressors. We must stay vigilant and be very careful of how we allow ourselves to be addressed.

We can too easily become what we are called with all the unwelcome responsibilities the title makes us heir to.

WHAT'S
SO FUNNY?

Some entertainers have tried to make art of their coarseness, but in their public crudeness they have merely revealed their own vast senses of personal inferiority. When they heap mud upon themselves and allow their tongues to wag with vulgarity, they expose their belief that they are not worth loving and are in fact unlovable. When we as audience indulge them in that profanity, we are not unlike Romans at a colosseum battle between unarmed Christians and raging lions. We not only participate in the humiliation of the entertainers, but are brought low by sharing in the obscenity.

We need to have the courage to say obesity is

not funny, vulgarity is not amusing, insolent children and submissive parents are not the characters we want to admire and emulate. Flippancy and sarcasm are not the only ways in which conversation can be conducted.

If the emperor is standing in my living room stripped to the buff, nothing should prevent me from saying that since he has no clothes on, he is not ready for public congress.

At any rate, not lounging on my sofa and munching on my trail mix.

DEATH
AND
THE LEGACY

When I think of death, and of late the idea has come with alarming frequency, I seem at peace with the idea that a day will dawn when I will no longer be among those living in this valley of strange humors. I can accept the idea of my own demise, but I am unable to accept the death of anyone else. I find it impossible to let a friend or relative go into that country of no return. Disbelief becomes my close companion, and anger follows in its wake.

I answer the heroic question "Death, where is thy sting?" with "It is here in my heart and mind and memories."

I am besieged with painful awe at the vacuum left by the dead. Where did she go? Where is she now? Are they, as the poet James Weldon Johnson said, "resting in the bosom of Jesus"? If so, what about my Jewish loves, my Japanese dears, and my Muslim darlings. Into whose bosom are they cuddled? There is always, lurking quietly, the question of what certainty is there that I, even I, will be gathered into the gentle arms of the Lord. I start to suspect that only with such blessed assurance will I be able to allow death its duties.

I find surcease from the entanglement of questions only when I concede that I am not obliged to know everything. In a world where many desperately seek to know all the answers, it is not very popular to believe, and then state, I do not need to know all things. I remind myself that it is sufficient that I know what I know and know that without believing that I will always know what I know or that what I know will always be true.

Also, when I sense myself filling with rage at the absence of a beloved, I try as soon as possible to remember that my concerns and questions, my efforts and answers should be focused on what I did or can learn from my departed love. What legacy was left which can help me in the art of living a good life?

If I employ the legacies of my late beloveds, I am certain death will take itself and me as well.

GETUPS

I was a twenty-one-year-old single parent with my son in kindergarten. Two jobs allowed me an apartment, food, and child care payment. Little money was left over for clothes, but I kept us nicely dressed in discoveries bought at the Salvation Army and other secondhand shops. Loving colors, I bought for myself beautiful reds and oranges, and greens and pinks, and teals and turquoise. I chose azure dresses and blouses and sweaters. And quite often I wore them in mixtures which brought surprise, to say the least, to the eyes of people who could not avoid noticing me. In fact, I concocted what southern black women used to call "getups."

Because I was very keen that my son not feel that he was neglected or different, I went frequently to his school. Sometimes between my jobs I would just go and stand outside the fenced play area. And he would, I am happy to say, always come and acknowledge me in the colorful regalia. I always wore beads. Lots of beads. The cheaper they were, the more I got, and sometimes I wore head wraps.

When my son was six and I twenty-two, he told me quite solemnly that he had to talk to me. We both sat down at the kitchen table, and he asked with an old man's eyes and a young boy's voice, "Mother, do you have any sweaters that match?" I was puzzled at first. I said, "No," and then I understood he was talking about the pullover and cardigan sets which were popular with white women. And I said, "No, I don't," maybe a little huffily. And he said, "Oh, I wish you did. So that you could wear them to school when you come to see me."

I was tickled, but I am glad I didn't laugh because he continued, "Mother, could you please only come to school when they call you?" Then I realized that my attire, which delighted my heart and certainly activated my creativity, was an embarrassment to him.

When people are young, they desperately need to conform, and no one can embarrass a young person in public so much as an adult to whom he or she is related. Any outré action or wearing of "getups" can make a young person burn with self-consciousness.

I learned to be a little more discreet to avoid causing him displeasure. As he grew older and more confident, I gradually returned to what friends thought of as my eccentric way of dressing. I was happier when I chose and created my own fashion.

I have lived in this body all my life and know it much better than any fashion designer. I think I know what looks good on me, and I certainly know what feels good in me.

I appreciate the creativity which is employed in the design of fabric and the design of clothes, and when something does fit my body and personality, I rush to it, buy it quickly, and wear it frequently. But I must not lie to myself for fashion's sake. I am only willing to purchase the item which becomes me and to wear that which enhances my image of myself to myself.

If I am comfortable inside my skin, I have the ability to make other people comfortable inside their skins although their feelings are not my primary reason for making my fashion choice. If I feel good inside my skin and clothes, I am thus free to allow my body its sway, its natural grace, its natural gesture. Then I am so comfortable that whatever I wear looks good on me even to the external fashion arbiters.

Dress is important to mention because many people are imprisoned by powerful dictates on what is right and proper to wear. Those decisions made by others and sometimes at their convenience are not truly meant to make life better or finer or more graceful or more gracious. Many times they stem from greed, insensitivity, and the need for control.

I have been in company, not long to be sure, but in company where a purveyor of taste will look at a woman or man who enters a room and will say with a sneer, "That was last year's jacket." As hastily as possible, I leave that company, but not before I record the snide attitude which has nothing to do with the beauty or effectiveness of the garment, but rather gives the speaker a moment's sense of superiority at, of course, someone else's expense.

Seek the fashion which truly fits and befits you. You will always be in fashion if you are true to yourself, and only if you are true to yourself. You might, of course, rightly wear that style which is emblazoned on the pages of the fashion magazines of the day, or you might not.

The statement "Clothes make the man" should be looked at, reexamined, and in fact reevaluated. Clothes can make the man or woman look silly and foppish and foolish. Try rather to be so much yourself that the clothes you choose increase your naturalness and grace.

LIVING WELL.
LIVING GOOD.

Aunt Tee was a Los Angeles member of our extended family. She was seventy-nine when I met her, sinewy, strong, and the color of old lemons. She wore her coarse, straight hair, which was slightly streaked with gray, in a long braided rope across the top of her head. With her high cheekbones, old gold skin, and almond eyes, she looked more like an Indian chief than an old black woman. (Aunt Tee described herself and any favored member of her race as Negroes. *Black* was saved for those who had incurred her disapproval.)

She had retired and lived alone in a dead, neat ground-floor apartment. Wax flowers and china figurines sat on elaborately embroidered and heavily starched doilies. Sofas and chairs were tautly upholstered. The only thing at ease in Aunt Tee's apartment was Aunt Tee.

I used to visit her often and perch on her uncomfortable sofa just to hear her stories. She was proud that after working thirty years as a maid, she spent the next thirty years as a live-in housekeeper, carrying the keys to rich houses and keeping meticulous accounts.

"Living in lets the white folks know Negroes are as neat and clean as they are, sometimes more so. And it gives the Negro maid a chance to see white folks ain't no smarter than Negroes. Just luckier. Sometimes."

Aunt Tee told me that once she was housekeeper for a couple in Bel Air, California, lived with them in a fourteen-room ranch house. There was a day maid who cleaned, and a gardener who daily tended the lush gardens. Aunt Tee oversaw the workers. When she had begun the job, she had cooked and served a light breakfast, a good lunch, and a full three- or four-course dinner to her employers and their guests. Aunt Tee said she watched them grow older and leaner. After a few years they stopped entertaining and ate dinner hardly seeing each other at the table. Finally, they sat in a dry silence as they ate evening meals of soft scrambled eggs, melba toast, and weak tea. Aunt Tee said she saw them growing old but didn't see herself aging at all.

She became the social maven. She started "keeping company" (her phrase) with a chauffeur down the street. Her best friend and her friend's husband worked in service only a few blocks away.

On Saturdays Aunt Tee would cook a pot of pigs' feet, a pot of greens, fry chicken, make potato salad, and bake a banana pudding. Then, that evening, her friends—the chauffeur, the other housekeeper, and her husband—would come to Aunt Tee's commodious live-in quarters. There the four would eat and drink, play records and dance. As the evening wore on, they would settle down to a serious game of bid whist.

Naturally, during this revelry jokes were told, fingers snapped, feet were patted, and there was a great deal of laughter.

Aunt Tee said that what occurred during every Saturday party startled her and her friends the first time it happened. They had been playing cards, and Aunt Tee, who had just won the bid, held a handful of trumps. She felt a cool breeze on her back and sat upright and turned around. Her employers had cracked her door open and beckoned to her. Aunt Tee, a little peeved, laid down her cards and went to the door. The couple backed away and asked her to come into the hall, and there they both spoke and won Aunt Tee's sympathy forever.

"Theresa, we don't mean to disturb you . . ." the man whispered, "but you all seem to be having such a good time . . ."

The woman added, "We hear you and your friends laughing every Saturday night, and we'd just like to watch you. We don't want to bother you. We'll be quiet and just watch."

The man said, "If you'll just leave your door ajar, your friends don't need to know. We'll never make a sound." Aunt Tee said she saw no harm in agreeing, and she talked it over with her company. They said it was OK with them, but it was sad that the employers owned the gracious house, the swimming pool, three cars, and numberless palm trees, but had no joy. Aunt Tee told me that laughter and relaxation had left the house; she agreed it was sad.

That story has stayed with me for nearly thirty years, and when a tale remains fresh in my mind,

it almost always contains a lesson which will benefit me.

My dears, I draw the picture of the wealthy
couple standing in a darkened hallway, peering into
a lighted room where black servants were lifting
their voices in merriment and comradery, and I
realize that living well is an art which can be developed. Of course, you will need the basic talents to
build upon: They are a love of life and ability to
take great pleasure from small offerings, an assurance that the world owes you nothing and that
every gift is exactly that, a gift. That people who
may differ from you in political stance, sexual per-
suasion, and racial inheritance can be founts of fun,
and if you are lucky, they can become even con-
vivial comrades.

Living life as art requires a readiness to forgive.
I do not mean that you should suffer fools gladly,
but rather remember your own shortcomings, and
when you encounter another with flaws, don't be
eager to righteously seal yourself away from the
offender forever. Take a few breaths and imagine
yourself having just committed the action which
has set you at odds.

Because of the routines we follow, we often
forget that life is an ongoing adventure. We leave

our homes for work, acting and even believing that we will reach our destinations with no unusual event startling us out of our set expectations. The truth is we know nothing, not where our cars will fail or when our buses will stall, whether our places of employment will be there when we arrive, or whether, in fact, we ourselves will arrive whole and alive at the end of our journeys. Life is pure adventure, and the sooner we realize that, the quicker we will be able to treat life as art: to bring all our energies to each encounter, to remain flexible enough to notice and admit when what we expected to happen did not happen. We need to remember that we are created creative and can invent new scenarios as frequently as they are needed.

Life seems to love the liver of it. Money and power can liberate only if they are used to do so. They can imprison and inhibit more finally than barred windows and iron chains.

WHEN
VIRTUE
BECOMES
REDUNDANT

Curious, but we have come to a place, a time, when virtue is no longer considered a virtue. The mention of virtue is ridiculed, and even the word itself has fallen out of favor. Contemporary writers rarely employ such words as *purity, temperance, goodness, worth,* or even *moderation*. Students, save those enrolled in philosophy courses or studying in seminaries, seldom encounter questions on morality and piety.

We need to examine what the absence of those qualities has done to our communal spirit, and we must learn how to retrieve them from the dust heap of nonuse and return them to a vigorous role in our lives.

Nature will not abide a vacuum, and because we have let the positive particulars go, they have been replaced with degeneracy, indifference, and vice. Our streets explode with cruelty and criminality, and our homes are rife with violence and abuse. Too many of our leaders shun the higher moral road and take the path to satisfy greed while they voice hollow rhetoric.

Everything costs and costs the earth. In order to win, we pay with energy and effort and discipline. If we lose, we pay in disappointment, discontent, and lack of fulfillment.

So, since a price will be exacted from us for everything we do or leave undone, we should pluck up the courage to win, to win back our finer and kinder and healthier selves.

I would like to see us go calling on the good example and upon virtue itself with the purpose of inviting them back into our conversations, our businesses, homes, and our lives, to reside in those places as favored friends.

POWER OF
THE
WORD

Many things continue to amaze me, even well into the sixth decade of my life. I'm startled or taken aback when people walk up to me and tell me they are Christians. My first response is the question "Already?" It seems to me a lifelong endeavor to try to live the life of a Christian. I believe that is also true for the Buddhist, for the Muslim, for the Jainist, for the Jew, and for the Taoist who try to live their beliefs. The idyllic condition cannot be arrived at and held on to eternally. It is in the search itself that one finds the ecstasy.

One of my earliest memories of Mamma, of my grandmother, is a glimpse of a tall cinnamon-colored woman with a deep, soft voice, standing thousands of feet up in the air on nothing visible. That incredible vision was a result of what my imagination would do each time Mamma drew herself up to her full six feet, clasped her hands behind her back, looked up into a distant sky, and said, "I will step out on the word of God."

The depression, which was difficult for everyone, especially so for a single black woman in the South tending her crippled son and two grandchildren, caused her to make the statement of faith often.

She would look up as if she could will herself into the heavens, and tell her family in particular and the world in general, "I will step out on the word of God. I will step out on the word of God." Immediately I could see her flung into space, moons at her feet and stars at her head, comets swirling around her. Naturally, since Mamma stood out on the word of God, and Mamma was over six feet tall, it wasn't difficult for me to have faith. I grew up knowing that the word of God had power.

In my twenties in San Francisco I became a sophisticate and an acting agnostic. It wasn't that I had stopped believing in God; it's just that God didn't seem to be around the neighborhoods I frequented. And then a voice teacher introduced me to *Lessons in Truth,* published by the Unity School of Christianity.

One day the teacher, Frederick Wilkerson, asked me to read to him. I was twenty-four, very erudite, very worldly. He asked that I read from *Lessons in Truth,* a section which ended with these words: "God loves me." I read the piece and closed the book, and the teacher said, "Read it again." I pointedly opened the book, and I sarcastically read, "God loves me." He said, "Again." After about the seventh repetition I began to sense that there might be truth in the statement, that there was a possibility that God really did love me. Me, Maya Angelou. I suddenly began to cry at the grandness of it all. I knew that if God loved me, then I could do wonderful things, I could try great things, learn anything, achieve anything. For what could stand against me with God, since one person, any person with God, constitutes the majority?

That knowledge humbles me, melts my bones, closes my ears, and makes my teeth rock loosely in their gums. And it also liberates me. I am a big bird winging over high mountains, down into serene valleys. I am ripples of waves on silver seas. I'm a spring leaf trembling in anticipation.

FURTHER
NEW
DIRECTIONS

Some people who exist sparingly on the mean side of the hill are threatened by those who also live in the shadows but who celebrate the light.

It seems easier to lie prone than to press against the law of gravity and raise the body onto its feet and persist in remaining vertical.

There are many incidents which can eviscerate the stalwart and bring the mighty down. In order to survive, the ample soul needs refreshments and reminders daily of its right to be and to be wherever it finds itself.

I was fired from a job when I was sixteen years old and was devastated. My entire personal worth was laid waste. My mother found me crying in my upstairs room. (I had left the door ajar, hoping for consolation.)

She tapped at the door and stepped in. When she asked why I was crying, I told her what happened.

Her face suddenly became radiant with indulgent smiles. She sat down on my bed and took me into her arms.

"Fired? Fired?" She laughed. "What the hell is that? Nothing. Tomorrow you'll go looking for another job. That's all."

She dabbed at my tears with her handkerchief. "So what? Remember, you were looking for a job when you found the one you just lost. So you'll just be looking for a job one more time."

She laughed at her wisdom and my youthful consternation. "And think about it, if you ever get fired again, the boss won't be getting a cherry. You've been through it once, and survived."

My mother, the late Vivian Baxter, retired from the merchant marine as a member of the Marine Cooks and Stewards Union. She practiced stepping off the expected road and cutting herself a brand-new path any time the desire arose. She inspired me to write the poem "Mrs. V. B."

Ships?
Sure I'll sail them.
Show me the boat,
If it'll float,
I'll sail it.

Men?
Yes I'll love them.
If they've got style,
To make me smile,
I'll love them.

Life?
'Course I'll live it.
Just enough breath,
Until my death,
And I'll live it.

Failure?
I'm not ashamed to tell it,
I never learned to spell it.
Not Failure.

COMPLAINING

When my grandmother was raising me in Stamps, Arkansas, she had a particular routine when people who were known to be whiners entered her store. Whenever she saw a known complainer coming, she would call me from whatever I was doing and say conspiratorially, "Sister, come inside. Come." Of course I would obey.

My grandmother would ask the customer, "How are you doing today, Brother Thomas?" And the person would reply, "Not so good." There would be a distinct whine in the voice. "Not so good today, Sister Henderson. You see, it's this summer. It's this summer heat. I just hate it. Oh, I hate it so much. It just frazzles me up and frazzles me down. I just hate the heat. It's almost killing me." Then my grandmother would stand stoically, her arms folded, and mumble, "Uh-huh, uh-huh." And she would cut her eyes at me to make certain that I had heard the lamentation.

At another time a whiner would mewl, "I hate plowing. That packed-down dirt ain't got no reasoning, and mules ain't got good sense. . . . Sure ain't. It's killing me. I can't ever seem to get done. My feet and my hands stay sore, and I get dirt in my eyes and up my nose. I just can't stand it." And my grandmother, again stoically with her arms folded, would say, "Uh-huh, uh-huh," and then look at me and nod.

As soon as the complainer was out of the store, my grandmother would call me to stand in front of her. And then she would say the same thing she had said at least a thousand times, it seemed to me. "Sister, did you hear what Brother So-and-So or Sister Much to Do complained about? You heard that?" And I would nod. Mamma would continue, "Sister, there are people who went to sleep all over the world last night, poor and rich and white and black, but they will never wake again. Sister, those who expected to rise did not, their beds became their cooling boards, and their blankets became their winding sheets. And those dead folks would give anything, anything at all for just five minutes of this weather or ten minutes of that plowing that person was grumbling about. So you watch yourself about complaining, Sister. What you're supposed to do when you don't like a thing is change it. If you can't change it, change the way you think about it. Don't complain."

It is said that persons have few teachable moments in their lives. Mamma seemed to have caught me at each one I had between the age of three and thirteen. Whining is not only graceless, but can be dangerous. It can alert a brute that a victim is in the neighborhood.

AT HARVESTTIME

There is an immutable life principle with which many people will quarrel.

Although nature has proven season in and season out that if the thing that is planted bears at all, it will yield more of itself, there are those who seem certain that if they plant tomato seeds, at harvesttime they can reap onions.

Too many times for comfort I have expected to reap good when I know I have sown evil. My lame excuse is that I have not always known that actions can only reproduce themselves, or rather, I have not always allowed myself to be aware of that knowledge. Now, after years of observation and enough courage to admit what I have observed, I try to plant peace if I do not want discord; to plant loyalty and honesty if I want to avoid betrayal and lies.

Of course, there is no absolute assurance that those things I plant will always fall upon arable land and will take root and grow, nor can I know if another cultivator did not leave contrary seeds before I arrived. I do know, however, that if I leave little to chance, if I am careful about the kinds of seeds I plant, about their potency and nature, I can, within reason, trust my expectations.

SENSUAL
ENCOURAGEMENT

We were young and lithe. Our brown bodies shone with heavy applications of baby oil and Max Factor theatrical makeup. Alvin Ailey and I were ardent students of Modern Dance, and when we could, we hired ourselves out as the dance team Al & Rita. Our most frequent employers were the secret and mysterious black organizations. When the Elks, the Masons, and the Eastern Stars gave socials, they always provided small bands, torch singers, and shake dancers for their membership.

Besides makeup, Alvin wore a leopard print G-string and I wore a homemade costume of a few feathers and even fewer sequins. We danced to Duke Ellington's "Caravan." Alvin had choreographed the routine, and he, as Pasha, would count out the first four bars of music, then leap from the dark onto the lighted stage. I, as the Pasha's dancing girl, would wait in the dark while he established the mood.

Inevitably, I would find women's hands on my body. Three or four would stroke my back, pat my behind, caress my arms. This was always accompanied by their whispers.

"That's right, honey. You're pretty. Go out there and shake that thang."

"When I was young, I used to shake it. I mean, shake it."

"Go on, baby. Get out there and drive him crazy."

So encouraged, I could barely await my cue, and when it did come, I would explode onto the stage and try to shake my brains out.

Looking back, I realize that the women's strokings were sensual rather than sexual. Because they encouraged me, they participated with me in the dance. Because they had enjoyed themselves when they were younglings, they did not envy me my youth.

Many adults show impatience with the young. They want them not only to grow up, but to grow old, and that immediately. They are quick to chide, criticize, and admonish:

"Be quiet."

"Sit down."

"Why are you always wiggling?"

"Keep still."

Whether consciously or not, those admonishments stem from a vigorous dissatisfaction with life and regret for a misspent youth.

VOICES
OF RESPECT

African Americans as slaves could not even claim to have won the names given to them in haste and given without a care, but they pridefully possessed a quality which modified the barbarism of their lives. They awoke before sunrise to be in the fields at first light and trudged back to floorless cabins in the evening's gloom. They had little chance for amicable exchange in the rows of cotton and the stands of sugarcane; still, they devised ways of keeping their souls robust and spirits alive in that awful atmosphere. They employed formally familial terms when addressing each other. Neither the slaveowner nor the slave overseer was likely to speak to a servant in anything but the cruelest language. But in the slave society Mariah became Aunt Mariah and Joe became Uncle Joe. Young girls were called Sister, Sis, or Tutta. Boys became brother, Bubba, and Bro and Buddy. It is true that those terms used throughout the slave communities had had their roots in the African worlds from which the slaves had been torn, but under bondage they began to have greater meaning and a more powerful impact. As in every society, certain tones of voice were and still are used to establish the quality of communication between the speaker and the person addressed. When African Americans choose to speak sweetly to each other, not only do the voices fall in register, but there is an unconscious increase in music between the speakers. In fact, a conversation between friends can sound as melodic as a scripted song.

We have used these terms to help us survive slavery, its aftermath, and today's crisis of revived racism. However, now, when too many children run mad in the land, and now, when we need courtesy as much as or more than ever, and when a little tenderness between people could make life more bearable, we are losing even the appearance of courtesy. Our youth, finding little or no courtesy at home, make exodus into streets filled with violent self-revulsion and an exploding vulgarity.

We must re-create an attractive and caring attitude in our homes and in our worlds. If our children are to approve of themselves, they must see that we approve of ourselves. If we persist in self-disrespect and then ask our children to respect themselves, it is as if we break all their bones and then insist that they win Olympic gold medals for the hundred-yard dash.

Outrageous.

EXTENDING
THE
BOUNDARIES

Terry's Pub was my pub, and it was the place to be if you were black and hip and in New York City. The bartenders were paragons of urban elegance, mixing and serving drinks smoothly and participating in conversations which ranged in subject matter from whether China should be allowed in the UN to the proper length of a micromini skirt.

The regulars were writers, models, high school principals, actors, journalists, movie actors, musicians, and college professors.

One afternoon I entered Terry's to find myself

surrounded by well-wishers with wide smiles and loud congratulations.

The bartender showed me the *New York Post* and then presented me with a huge martini. I was featured as the newspaper's "Person of the Week." The regulars suspended their usual world-weary demeanor, giving hearty compliments, which I accepted heartily.

Eventually the toasters returned to their tables and I was left to grow gloomy in silence. Moodiness and a creeping drunkenness from too many martinis dimmed the room and my spirits.

Here, in my finest hour, I was alone. What had I done to any man to make him want to leave me and, even worse, not to win me to his side in the first place?

The questions came in the order of a military phalanx. Each marched into my consciousness, was recognized, and proceeded to make way for the next. I ordered another martini and resolved to soberly answer the inquiries. I was forty-one years old, slender, tall, and was often thought to be around thirty. No one had ever called me beautiful, save the odd Africanist who told me I looked like an African statue. Having seen many Yoruba and Fon wooden sculptures, I was not lured into believing myself anything but rather plain. I did dress strikingly and walked straight, my head evenly upon my shoulders, so kind people often said of me, "That's a handsome woman."

But here I was between affairs and alone. Like many women, I did regard the absence of a romantic liaison as a stigma which showed me unlovable.

I sat at the bar, mumbling over my inadequacies and drinking at least the fifth martini, when my roving eye fell on a table. Near the window sat five young, smart, black male journalists enjoying each other's company. They had been among the people who crowded around me earlier when the day had been bright, my present glorious, and my future assured. But they also had retreated, gone back to the comfort of their own table.

A tear slipped down my cheek. I called the bartender to settle my bill, but he informed me that all had been taken care of, anonymously. With that pronouncement of kindness before me and the self-pitying thoughts behind me, I gathered my purse and, removing myself from the stool, gingerly pointed myself in the direction of the journalists' table. The men looked up, saw my drunkenness, and became alarmed and guarded.

I pulled a chair from another table and asked, "Do you mind if I join you?"

I sat and looked at each man for a long time, and then I began a performance which now, more than twenty years later, can still cause me to seriously consider changing my name and my country of residence.

I asked of the table at large, "What is wrong with me? I know I'm not pretty, but I'm not the ugliest woman in the world. And if I was, I'd still deserve having a man of my own."

I began to list my virtues.

"I keep a beautiful house, tables polished, fresh flowers, even if daisies, at least once a week.

"I'm an excellent cook.

"I can manage my house and an outside job without keeling over in a dead faint.

"I enjoy sex and have what I hope is a normal appetite.

"I can speak French and Spanish, some Arabic and Fanti, and I read all the papers and journals and a book a week so that I can share an intelligent conversation with you.

"And none of all that appeals to you?"

I raised my voice. "Do you mean to tell me that that's not enough for you?"

The men were embarrassed and angry with themselves at being embarrassed. Angry with me for having brought such unwieldy, drunken, awkward questions to their table.

In one second I realized that I had done just what they feared of me. That I had overstepped the unwritten rules which I knew I should have respected. Instead, I had brazenly and boldly come to their table and spoken out on, of all things, loneliness.

When I realized my intoxication, I started to cry. An acquaintance at the bar walked over to our silent table. He greeted the men and asked, "Maya, sister, can I walk you home?" I looked up into his dark brown face and began to recover. His presence seemed to sober me a little. I found a handkerchief in my purse, and without rushing, I dabbed my face. I stood up and away from the table. I said, "Good-bye, gentlemen," and took my rescuer's hand. We walked out of the bar.

The long block to home was made longer by my companion's disapproving sounds. He clucked his tongue and muttered. "You shouldn't be drinking martinis. Especially by yourself." I didn't have the will to remind him that I thought I had been with friends.

He continued. . . . "You draw people to you; then you push them away."

I sure didn't have to push the journalists away.

"You give that big smile and act like you're just waiting for a man to take you in his arms, but then you freeze up like an iceberg. . . . People don't know how to take you." Well, they must not. I hadn't been taken.

We arrived at my apartment, and I gave my attendant the sweetest, briefest smile I had in me and stepped inside and closed the door.

I entered into a long concentration which lasted until and even after I sobered myself.

At the end of my meditation I came to understand that I had been looking for love, but only under specific conditions. I was looking for a mate, but he had to be a certain color, he had to have a certain intellect. I had standards. It was just likely that my standards eliminated a number of possibilities.

I had married a Greek in my green youth, and the marriage had ended poorly, so I had not consciously thought of accepting any more advances from outside my own race. The real reason, or I think another reason, for not including non–

African Americans in my target area was that I knew that if it was difficult to sustain a love affair between people who had grown up next door and who looked alike and whose parents had attended church together, how much more so between people from different races who had so few things in common.

However, during that afternoon and evening I arrived at the conclusion that if a man came along who seemed to me to be honest and sincere, who wanted to make me laugh and succeeded in doing so, a man who had a lilting spirit—if such a man came along who had a respect for other human beings, then if he was Swedish, African, or a Japanese sumo wrestler, I would certainly give him my attention, and I would not struggle too hard if he caught me in a web of charm.

BRUTALITY
IS DEFINITELY
NOT ACCEPTABLE

Certain phrases excite and alarm me. That is, when I hear them, I respond as if I have smelled gas escaping in a closed room. Without having to think of my next move, if I am not hemmed in, I make my way toward the handiest exit. If I cannot escape, however, I react defensively.

"Don't mind me, I'm brutally frank." That is always a summons to arms.

I recognize the timid sadist who would like to throw a stone and hide her hand or, better, who would like not only to wound but to be forgiven by the soon-to-be-injured even before the injury.

Well, I do mind brutality in any of its guises, and I will not be lured into accepting it merely because the brute asks me to do so.

"I hope you won't take this the wrong way . . ." is another bell ringer for me.

I sense the mealymouthed attacker approaching so if I cannot flee, I explain in no uncertain voice if there is even the slightest chance that I might take a statement the wrong way, be assured that I will do so. I advise the speaker that it would be better to remain silent than to try to collect the speaker's bruised feelings, which I intend to leave in pieces scattered on the floor.

I am never proud to participate in violence, yet I know that each of us must care enough for ourselves to be ready and able to come to our own self-defense.

OUR BOYS

The plague of racism is insidious, entering into our minds as smoothly and quietly and invisibly as floating airborne microbes enter into our bodies to find lifelong purchase in our bloodstreams.

Here is a dark little tale which exposes the general pain of racism. I wrote ten one-hour television programs called *Blacks, Blues, Blacks*, which highlighted Africanisms still current in American life. The work was produced in San Francisco at KQED.

The program "African Art's Impact in Western Art" was fourth in the series. In it I planned to show the impact African sculpture had on the art of Picasso, Modigliani, Paul Klee, and Rouault. I learned that a Berkeley collector owned many pieces of East African Makonde sculpture. I contacted the collector, who allowed me to select thirty pieces of art. When they were arranged on lighted plinths, the shadows fell from the sculptures on to the floor, and we photographed them in dramatic sequence. The collector and his wife were so pleased with the outcome that at my farewell dinner they presented me with a piece of sculpture as a memento. They were white, older, amused and amusing. I knew that if I lived in their area, we would become social friends.

I returned to New York, but three years later I moved back to Berkeley to live. I telephoned the collector and informed him of my move. He said, "So glad you called. I read of your return in the newspaper. Of course we must get together." He went on, "You know I am the local president of the National Council of Christians and Jews. But you don't know what I've been doing since we last spoke. I've been in Germany trying to ameliorate the conditions for the American soldiers." His voice was weighted with emotion. He said, "You know, the black soldiers are having a horrific time over there, and our boys are having a hard time, too."

I asked, "What did you say?"

He said, "Well, I'm saying that the black soldiers are having it particularly rough, but our guys are having a bad time, too."

I asked, "Would you repeat that?"

He said, "Well, I'm saying . . ." Then his mind played back his statement, or he reheard the echo of his blunder hanging in the air.

He said, "Oh, my God, I've made such a stupid mistake, and I'm speaking to Maya Angelou." He said, "I'm so embarrassed, I'm going to hang up." I said, "Please don't. Please don't. This incident merely shows how insidious racism is. Please, let's talk about it." I could hear embarrassment in his voice, and hesitations and chagrin. Finally, after about three or four minutes, he managed to hang up. I telephoned him three times, but he never returned my telephone calls.

The incident saddened and burdened me. The man, his family and friends were lessened by not getting to know me and my family and friends. And it also meant that I, my family, and my friends were lessened by not getting to know him. Because we never had a chance to talk, to teach each other and learn from each other, racism had diminished all the lives it had touched.

It is time for the preachers, the rabbis, the priests and pundits, and the professors to believe in the awesome wonder of diversity so that they can teach those who follow them. It is time for parents to teach young people early on that in diversity there is beauty and there is strength. We all should know that diversity makes for a rich tapestry, and we must understand that all the threads of the tapestry are equal in value no matter their color; equal in importance no matter their texture.

Our young must be taught that racial peculiarities do exist, but that beneath the skin, beyond the differing features and into the true heart of being, fundamentally, we are more alike, my friend, than we are unalike.

> . . . Mirror twins are different
> although their features jibe,
> and lovers think quite different
> thoughts
> while lying side by side.
>
> We love and lose in China,
> we weep on England's moors,
> and laugh and moan in Guinea,
> and thrive on Spanish shores.

We seek success in Finland,
are born and die in Maine.
In minor ways we differ,
in major we're the same.

I note the obvious differences
between each sort and type,
but we are more alike, my friends,
than we are unalike.

We are more alike, my friends,
than we are unalike.
We are more alike, my friends,
than we are unalike.

JEALOUSY

A jealous lover can be a little amusing. In fact, jealousy made evident in a room filled with people can be an outright intoxicant to everyone, including the lovers. It must be remembered, however, that jealousy in romance is like salt in food. A little can enhance the savor, but too much can spoil the pleasure and, under certain circumstances, can be life-threatening.

PLANNED
PREGNANCY

The woman who has the fortune to plan a pregnancy also has the opportunity to experience rare pleasures. She can consciously participate in the evolution of her body from fecundity to its ultimate production stage, the delivery of a child. During the entire period, if she remains attentive, she will marvel at the emergence of new and delightful sensualities.

She must carefully prepare her mind in order to enjoy the parturition. She will spend time appreciating her body before conception. Knowing that her features will undergo dramatic changes, she and her mate will spend considerable time examining and enjoying her breasts and calves and arms and belly.

She will have photographs made for the months ahead, which will seem to stretch into years. When her belly extends so far that her feet disappear from her view, then the portraits of her lissome days will have the value of rare gems.

If she and her mate do not consider pregnancy a common occurrence just because it happens all the time, if they are persistently imaginative, each stage can furnish them exquisite gratification.

A
DAY AWAY

We often think that our affairs, great or small, must be tended continuously and in detail, or our world will disintegrate, and we will lose our places in the universe. That is not true, or if it is true, then our situations were so temporary that they would have collapsed anyway.

Once a year or so I give myself a day away. On the eve of my day of absence, I begin to unwrap the bonds which hold me in harness. I inform housemates, my family and close friends that I will not be reachable for twenty-four hours; then I disengage the telephone. I turn the radio dial to an all-music station, preferably one which plays the soothing golden oldies. I sit for at least an hour in a very hot tub; then I lay out my clothes in preparation for my morning escape, and knowing that nothing will disturb me, I sleep the sleep of the just.

On the morning I wake naturally, for I will have set no clock, nor informed my body timepiece when it should alarm. I dress in comfortable shoes and casual clothes and leave my house going no place. If I am living in a city, I wander streets, window-shop, or gaze at buildings. I enter and leave public parks, libraries, the lobbies of skyscrapers, and movie houses. I stay in no place for very long.

On the getaway day I try for amnesia. I do not want to know my name, where I live, or how many dire responsibilities rest on my shoulders. I detest encountering even the closest friend, for then I am reminded of who I am, and the circumstances of my life, which I want to forget for a while.

Every person needs to take one day away. A day in which one consciously separates the past from the future. Jobs, lovers, family, employers, and friends can exist one day without any one of us, and if our egos permit us to confess, they could exist eternally in our absence.

Each person deserves a day away in which no problems are confronted, no solutions searched for. Each of us needs to withdraw from the cares which will not withdraw from us. We need hours of aimless wandering or spates of time sitting on park benches, observing the mysterious world of ants and the canopy of treetops.

If we step away for a time, we are not, as many may think and some will accuse, being irresponsible, but rather we are preparing ourselves to more ably perform our duties and discharge our obligations.

When I return home, I am always surprised to find some questions I sought to evade had been answered and some entanglements I had hoped to flee had become unraveled in my absence.

A day away acts as a spring tonic. It can dispel rancor, transform indecision, and renew the spirit.

Also by Maya Angelou

I KNOW WHY THE CAGED BIRD SINGS

'Verve, nerve and joy in her own talents effervesce throughout this book' *–Julia O'Faolain*

'Its humour, even in the face of appalling discrimination, is robust. Autobiographical writing at its very best' *–Philip Oakes*

In this first volume of her extraordinary autobiography, Maya Angelou beautifully evokes her childhood in the American South of the 1930s. She and her brother live with their grandmother, in Stamps, Arkansas, where Maya learns the power of the 'whitefolks' at the other end of town. A visit to her adored mother ends in tragedy when Maya is raped by her mother's lover. But her extraordinary sense of wholeness emerges; she discovers the pleasures of dance and drama and gives birth to a treasured son.

GATHER TOGETHER IN MY NAME

'She has warmth and humour and a sense of wholeness and content that glows through' – Polly Toynbee, *Guardian*

'Remarkable, devoid of bitterness; pungent; funny ... with that rare gift for hope in adversity' – Fiona Maddocks, *New Statesman*

In this moving sequel to her bestselling *I Know Why The Caged Bird Sings*, the war is over and Maya has given birth to a son. Unemployed, isolated, she embarks on a series of brief lonely affairs and transient jobs – in shops, restaurants and nightclubs. Finally she turns to prostitution and the world of narcotics. But even in great adversity, Maya Angelou invests life with the remarkable sense of richness that has won her such an enormous following.

SINGIN' AND SWINGIN' AND GETTIN' MERRY LIKE CHRISTMAS

'She sees everything with an eye full of relish'
– Hilary Bailey, *Guardian*

'I know that not since the days of my childhood, when people in books were more real than the people one saw every day, have I found myself so moved' – James Baldwin

At twenty-one Maya Angelou's life has a double focus – music and her son. Working in a record store to support both, she is on the edge of new worlds: marriage, show business and, in 1954, a triumphant tour of Europe and North Africa as feature dancer with *Porgy and Bess*. There are setbacks and disappointments, but energy and a profound confidence in her ability to survive keep Maya buoyant. A joyful celebration of music and dance, travel and friendship, this is the third volume of Maya Angelou's marvellous autobiography.

THE HEART OF A WOMAN

'The freshness of Maya Angelou's writing is something to marvel at' – Philip Oakes

'Loving the world, Maya Angelou also knows its cruelty and offers up her autobiography as an extraordinary mixture of innocence and depravity, of elegy and celebration' – Nicci Gerrard, *New Statesman*

In the fourth volume of her enthralling autobiography, Maya Angelou leaves California for a new life in New York, where she becomes immersed in the world of Black writers and artists in Harlem. Increasingly active in the Black rights movement, she is appointed Northern Coordinator to Martin Luther King. Her personal life is as tempestuous as ever: swept off her feet by Vusumzi Make, South African freedom fighter, she marries him after a whirlwind courtship. They go to Egypt, where the marriage fails but her career blossoms. Holding the book together is Maya's absorbing account of her relationship with her son, as, with pain and joy, she watches him grow up to find his own identity.

ALL GOD'S CHILDREN NEED TRAVELLING SHOES

'She continues with all the freshness and warmth of her earlier books' – *Evening Standard*

'Maya Angelou has an amazing ability to take readers into her personal maze and lead them out again feeling refreshed and even jubilant' – Clancy Sigal, *Guardian*

In the fifth volume of her brilliant autobiography Maya Angelou emigrates to Ghana, only to discover that 'you can't go home again'. Initially she experiences the joy of being Black in a Black country, certain that Africa must be her Promised Land. But Ghana leads its own paradoxical life: she finds official sexism but loving female friendships; Black solidarity but distrust of Black Americans. Through the circumstances of her new life – an affair with a seductive Malian, her son's near-tragic accident, politics, partying – her myth of 'Mother Africa' is dismantled. Encountering the country on its own terms, she comes to a new awareness of herself, of slavery and Black betrayal, of civil rights and mothering.

Poetry by Maya Angelou

AND STILL I RISE

'It is true poetry she is writing . . . it has an innate purity about it, unquenchable dignity' – M.F.K. Fisher

Maya Angelou's poetry – lyrical and dramatic, exuberant and playful – speaks of love, longing, partings; of Saturday night partying, and the smells and sounds of Southern cities; of freedom and shattered dreams. 'The caged bird sings/with a fearful trill/ of things unknown/but longed for still/and his tune is heard/on the distant hill/for the caged bird/sings of freedom.' Of her poetry, *Kirkus Reviews* has written, 'It is just as much a part of her autobiography as *I Know Why the Caged Bird Sings, Gather Together in My Name, Singin' and Swingin' and Gettin' Merry Like Christmas, Heart of a Woman* and *All God's Children Need Travelling Shoes*'.

Also available:
JUST GIVE ME A COOL DRINK OF WATER 'FORE I DIIIE
I SHALL NOT BE MOVED
ON THE PULSE OF MORNING
THE COMPLETE COLLECTED POEMS OF MAYA ANGELOU

EVEN THE STARS LOOK LONESOME

'America's unofficial Poet Laureate waxes lyrical' –
Cosmopolitan

There is no one quite like Maya Angelou. Poet to the president, champion of the people, best-selling autobiographer, her experiences as dancer, singer, waitress, activist, director, teacher, wife and mother, have made her one of the few people truly qualified to share her lessons of a lifetime. With her customary courage and humour – and always with style and grace – she reflects on the people and places she has known. She talks about Africa and ageing, she gives us a profile on her great friend and 'daughter' Oprah Winfrey, she sings the praises of sensuality. But here too are her thoughts on the end of a much-wanted marriage, confessions of rage and the importance of solitude.

Lucas Pau Pau - (Roddar)

Now you can order superb titles directly from Virago

- [ ] I Know Why the Caged Bird Sings   Maya Angelou   £6.99
- [ ] Gather Together in My Name   Maya Angelou   £6.99
- [ ] Singin' and Swingin' and Gettin' Merry Like
Christmas   Maya Angelou   £6.99
- [ ] The Heart of a Woman   Maya Angelou   £6.99
- [ ] All God's Children Need Travelling Shoes   Maya Angelou   £6.99
- [ ] Even the Stars Look Lonesome   Maya Angelou   £5.99
- [ ] And Still I Rise   Maya Angelou   £8.99

Please allow for postage and packing: **Free UK delivery.**
Europe; add 25% of retail price; Rest of World; 45% of retail price.

To order any of the above or any other Virago titles, please call our credit card orderline or fill in this coupon and send/fax it to:

Virago, 250 Western Avenue, London, W3 6XZ, UK.
Fax 0181 324 5678   Telephone 0181 324 5516

- [ ] I enclose a UK bank cheque made payable to Virago for £ ....
- [ ] Please charge £.............. to my Access, Visa, Delta, Switch Card No.

☐☐☐☐☐☐☐☐☐☐☐☐☐☐☐☐☐☐☐

Expiry Date ☐☐☐☐   Switch Issue No. ☐☐

NAME (Block letters please) ....

ADDRESS ....

....

....

Postcode ....Telephone ....

Signature ....

Please allow 28 days for delivery within the UK. Offer subject to price and availability.

Please do not send any further mailings from companies carefully selected by Virago ☐